The Bread Book

The Bread Book

Debbie Boater

Prism Press

Published in 1979 by
PRISM PRESS
Stable Court
Chalmington
Dorchester
Dorset DT2 0HB

© Copyright Debbie Boater 1979

ISBN Hardback 0 904727 95 5
ISBN Paperback 0 904727 96 3

Printed in Great Britain by
McCorquodale (Newton) Ltd
Newton Le Willows, Merseyside

Contents

Acknowledgements

Illustrations by Trevor Aldous

The Author wishes to thank Dr. C. Clutterbuck and John Clark of the British Society for Social Responsibility in Science, 9 Poland Street, London W.1

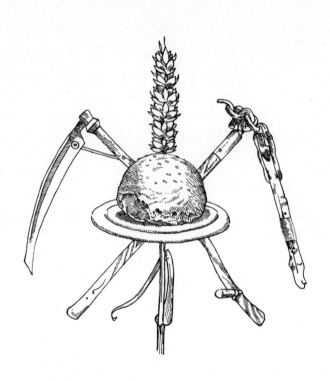

Introduction

Bread is our most important food, our principal food. On average we each eat 4–6 slices a day. And yet we know so very little about it. How many of us know what goes into bread, how it is made, what effect it has upon us? This book is aimed at answering such questions.

Whilst on the one hand it is being increasingly admitted that there are great gaps in our understanding of nutrition, most especially in the relationship between nutrition and both physical and mental health, on the other hand, little or nothing of this subject is taught in our schools. Information that is available to the general public is often confusing and lacking in the practical help so often needed that only direct tuition can give.

The Wholefood School of Nutrition publishes a bi-monthly magazine, Wholefood News & Views, and has established a small but growing network of teachers, spread out across the country. Working in their own areas, these teachers organise and run courses that cover the use of grains, pulses, nuts, seeds, vegetables and seaweeds; as well as a basic understanding of nutrition and how the preparation and cooking of food is one of the most important activities of our lives.

Chapter I

A History of Milling and Baking

There is no doubt that bread, in one form or another, has always been the principal food in man's diet, his 'staff of life'. Grains have been eaten for over 100,000 years; cultivated and ground into flour for over 10,000 years. Gradually, through the ages, different milling and baking techniques have developed, although there was comparatively little development up until the Industrial Revolution, compared to the change that this, and subsequent technology have brought. Previously, all flour was stone-ground, whether in a small grinder, with a round rolling-stone or between two flat stones, one of which was powered by water, wind or rotated by horses. The Industrial Revolution brought with it the steel roller, a completely different method of milling which not only changed the type of flour produced, but also radically changed the eating habits of the nation.

The most favoured grain for making bread has always been wheat, as it was seen to make the lightest of breads, bread that was well-risen from a dough that was easy to handle. This is mainly because wheat contains a high proportion of gluten, combined with a cellulose structure that holds together well. Other grains, such as corn or rye, have been used and in some countries are still used more than wheat, but they contain less gluten and therefore tend to make a heavier, flatter bread. In the past, the use of wheat was much associated with status, being the most expensive grain, with the poorer classes being dependent on rye, oats and barley for their flour. Leavened breads were made, baked on the hearth or in wood stoves and eaten as the main food of the day. Some breads were leavened with yeast, others with a natural leavener, made from sour dough.

In certain areas, oatcakes were the staple bread, especially in areas where wheat did not grow well, such as the North of England. There is an idea that oatcakes were first introduced by the Viking settlers and in some areas they are still known as Havercakes, 'haver' being the old Norse word for oats. They used to be made on a bakestone, originally of a soft stone that was split and hardened by heat, then iron bakestones were used or griddles suspended over an open fire. Nowadays, gas fired iron hot-plates are most common. The bakers used special implements to shape and throw the cakes onto the hot-plates, after which they were dried on a rack until crisp and hard.

The desire to 'whiten' or refine flour goes back some 2,000 years to the Roman aristocracy, who ate bread made from sifted, or sieved flour, whitened with small amounts of chalk. This flour was similar to what we can buy today as 85% extraction flour, as it still retained the germ, and only the larger particles of the flour were sifted out (the bran). This practice set a pattern and white flour became the most sought after, associated with wealth and purity, thereby creating a craving in those unable to afford it. Families were even known to forgo other foods in order to be able to buy white bread and by the end of the eighteenth century, sales of brown bread were virtually non-existent in the towns, with wholewheat bread only surviving in the rural areas where bread was still home baked.

With the Industrial Revolution came the need to increase bread production as towns rapidly grew in size. The milling industry had many problems, one of the biggest being that of storage. Flour that is stone-ground has the germ of the grain milled in with the rest of the flour, thus the essential oils stored in the germ are evenly distributed throughout the flour. This oil, once exposed to oxygen, will start to oxidise, and will go rancid within 4–6 months. So the storage, or 'life' of the flour, was limited.

The steel roller mills that were introduced in the 1870's provided the answer, by firstly splitting the grain, before milling, and enabling it to then be sieved and separated into three different products —the bran, the germ and the endosperm, which is the main part of the grain and which is milled into white flour. The advantages of this method to the miller were enormous. Firstly, the resulting flour was whiter (therefore 'purer') as both the germ and the bran had been fully extracted; secondly, in removing the germ before grinding the flour, it meant that no oil from the germ passed into the flour, therefore there was no risk of the flour going rancid, it now had indefinite 'life'; thirdly, the flour could be milled finer and more evenly between steel rollers than it could between stones, thus producing a more standardised flour; fourthly, the miller now had two other products — the bran and the germ — that could be sold off separately for extra profit, usually as animal food. Thus, for the first time, white flour became the common flour, cheaper than brown and the only form of bread that most millers made. In the space of a few years a complete turnabout had taken place from the days when only brown bread was made. It also meant that the main food in our diet has become extremely low in essential nutrients.

Although the milling of flour was now firmly established in factories with big steel rollers, the making of bread still contained a few problems, one of them being the type of wheat used. English wheat contains very little gluten compared to wheat grown in Canada and the U.S.A. Dependent on the type of wheat used is the ability of the bread to rise well and the finished texture of the bread, but the biggest difficulty of all was the time factor — bread took up to three hours to make.

This difficulty was not resolved in England until the 1960's with the invention of what is called the Chorleywood Bread Process (CBP), a process which is now responsible for most of the bread made and sold in bakeries and supermarkets, with similar methods used in America. It is a mixing process that speeds up the dough making to only a few minutes, thereby changing the structure of the gluten in the flour so that the bread rises well even without yeast. It also means that the water content in the loaf can be increased considerably, thus increasing the amount of bread produced per pound of flour. . . .

Today's Bread and its Additives

Milling flour and baking bread is a major part of the food industry, with two large groups controlling over 70% of bread sales in Britain (Ranks Hovis McDougall and Associated British Foods) and four large groups in the U.S.A. (ITT, Campbell-Taggart, American Baking and Interstate Brands) with some smaller plant bakeries and independent master bakers who bake and sell on their own premises. The making of bread is often associated in our minds with happy, rosy cheeked bakers and an enticing smell, as is often the case with the master bakers. But this is not so with the big bread companies. Responsible for vast quantities of bread eaten each day, sold under various brand names in bakery shops and supermarkets, these companies are also involved in many allied concerns such as animal feedstuffs, meat processing and packaging (having fed the animals with the separated bran and germ . . .), butter and cheese making, agricultural machinery, pet foods, supermarket chains, as well as numerous biscuit and cake products. It is a massive industry with one company in America spending up to 5 million dollars a year on TV advertising.

As these companies are so big, they obviously wield a great deal of power, thereby dictating somewhat the type of products that reach the public. So here we can see clearly that much of the food on the shelves in the shops is not there because it is good for us nutritionally, nor has it necessarily been prepared in such a way as to preserve the nutrients. It is there to make money, any products that do not make money are removed.

As with all processed foods, it is more than just the original food that goes into the finished product. Additives to flour and bread are numerous, some at best are questionable and at worst could be harmful. The main reason for most of the chemical additives is to change the wheat molecules, thereby changing the structure of the wheat, in order to produce a 'better' loaf, one that will rise more and be of a more uniform shape, but not better in its value as food. What is not known, however, is the long term effect this change may have on those who eat such altered wheat. After all, for thousands of years we have been eating unaltered, whole wheat — only very recently have these changes come into practice. And there is evidence to show that when a food is radically changed, the nutritional content and the effect on our health is also changed.

To produce the pure white flour we are all familiar with, it has to be bleached or it would be a grey-yellowy colour. In the past fine chalk was used, more recently it was agene. Nowadays a number of different bleaches are added, although in Britain it is mainly chlorine dioxide. The bleaching also 'improves' the flour, or rather speeds up the maturing process, thus apparently making it easier for bread making. Chlorine dioxide is kept behind sealed doors and millers who use it wear head-to-toe protective clothing. Quite a few other countries also use chlorine dioxide although in France there is a ban on its use. The bleaching process not only whitens and matures the flour, it also destroys much of its nutritional content, especially vitamin E.

Each country has its own list of permitted additives. In Britain the following may be added to white bread:

1 bleaching agent   4 emulsifiers
9 improving agents   1 colour
4 preservatives   4 nutrients
5 anti-oxidents

Some of the chemicals are: ascorbic acid, benzoyl peroxide, sulphur dioxide, potassium bromate. Anti-oxidents include butylated hydroxy-tolune (BHT) which was recommended for discontinuation in 1963 but is still in use, despite the fact that it is banned in some other countries and has been found to have harmful side-effects in animal tests, i.e. enlarged livers and mental disturbance.

In the U.S.A. a similar list applies although it is slightly different as the methods of making the bread differ, i.e. the CBP method used in Britain requires the addition of oil which requires an anti-oxident (BHT). But the list of additives in American bread is often a much longer one, bakers can apply to add extra additives as long as they can prove their safety. In one instance a loaf was found to have up to 93 added ingredients!

Many of the additives, especially the anti-oxidents and preservatives, are there to enable the bread to keep its fresh appearance from the factory to the shop, which in certain cases can be quite a long time, without the fats going rancid or the bread going dry. This becomes more necessary as the bread industry becomes more concentrated and less localised. We shall examine the use of the added nutrients in the next chapter. The colour that is added is usually caramel, necessary because many of the 'brown' breads on sale are made with white flour, with a small amount of bran or germ added for extra texture and caramel to colour it brown. If you ask for a wholemeal loaf, you should get one, i.e. a loaf made with 100% wholewheat flour. But this may not happen as many bakers either do not know the difference or do not distinguish between wholewheat and brown. A wheatmeal loaf should be made from 80–85% extraction flour but it is often found to be the same as a brown loaf, that is, made from white flour and caramel.

The mass manufacture of bread is now the norm, as was once the home-baking of bread. White bread sales account for 85–90% of all bread sold. But nutritionally it is at last being recognised that refined white flour and bread is not as beneficial as wholewheat or unrefined flour and can possibly even be said to be harmful over a long period of time, due to the lack of natural nutrients, fibre and the addition of so many chemicals.

Chapter II

Nutrition and Bread

Over the past few years there has been increasing medical concern over the amount of refined foods we eat, in particular refined cereals, i.e. white flour and bread. White refined flour is not a natural food, having been changed considerably from its original state, and as such it is not surprising that illnesses, often serious, may occur from consuming it in large quantities. Our bodies have not evolved to be able to cope adequately with refined carbohydrates without causing some damage. On average we eat 6 slices of bread a day, as well as an ever increasing amount of cakes and biscuits, made with white flour and white sugar. Up to 50% of our diet (more amongst those on a low income) may be made up of these foods, which contain little nutritional value at all. All whole grains provide a balanced and necessary supply of nutrients, 'nature's package deal', in a form that is easily digested and doesn't overburden the system. Taking wheat as an example, we can see what it has to offer us:

THE BRAN: Basically this is what has come to be known as roughage or fibre. This is because the bran is largely made up of cellulose which the body cannot fully break down and so it passes through the body partly undigested, thus adding extra bulk or roughage. More of this later. Bran also contains a considerable amount of nutriment, in the form of vitamin B, iron and a little protein.

THE GERM: The power house of the grain, the smallest yet most nutritious

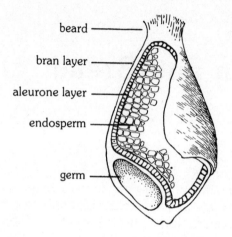

beard

bran layer

aleurone layer

endosperm

germ

part of the grain, rich in vitamins B and E, iron and other minerals, essential unsaturated fat and protein.

THE ENDOSPERM: This is the main body of the grain, the food supply that the germ lives off when it is growing and which is mainly made up of carbohydrate in the form of starch with some protein, particularly gluten. It is this part of the grain that is made into white flour.

As a whole grain, these nutrients work together. For instance, vitamin B, found mainly in the germ and the bran, is necessary for the full utilisation of the carbohydrate in the endosperm. Separate the grain and these nutrients can no longer operate together, nutritionally they become far less valuable. Consequently, since the 1940's when it was recognised that white bread was not nutritionally adequate, certain nutrients have been added to white bread, in an attempt to restore some of the nutritive value of the original grain. But the original grain contained up to 24 different nutrients, out of which only a handful survive the refining process, with even these severely reduced in quantity. Only 5 are required to be replaced, in a chemical form. These are iron, calcium, vitamins B1, B2 and niacin. But as can be seen from the chart below, there is still a big difference between wholewheat flour and refined flour, even with added nutrients.

Vitamin and mineral loss in the refining of wholewheat to produce 70% extraction rate white flour:

Nutrient	loss in flour %
Thiamine (vit B1)	77.1
Riboflavine (vit B2)	80.0
Niacin	80.8
Vitamin B6	71.8
Pantothenic acid	50.0
Alpha-tocopheral (vit E)	86.3
Calcium	60.0
Phosphorous	70.9
Magnesium	84.7
Potassium	77.0
Sodium	78.3
Chromium	40.0
Manganese	85.8
Iron	75.6
Cobalt	88.5
Copper	67.9
Zinc	77.7
Selenium	15.9

From Schroeder H. 'Losses of vitamins and trace minerals resulting from processing and refining of foods', *American Journal of Clinical Nutrition* No. 24, May 1971.

A few words about the nutrients that are replaced:

Iron
Iron is an essential nutrient, necessary for the formation of red blood cells and the transportation of oxygen. A lack of it can cause anaemia, especially

at times of heavy blood loss or pregnancy. We obtain iron from a great number of different foods: eggs, meat, green vegetables, dried fruits, molasses and whole grains, to name but a few. Excess iron can lead to iron deposits in the liver, causing a variety of different ailments. Iron deficiency is actually quite rare (anaemia can be caused by a number of things, not just a lack of iron) and it is felt to be quite unnecessary to add extra to bread. Also, it has now been found that the form of iron added cannot be fully absorbed in the body.

Calcium

Calcium is necessary, along with phosphorous, for the development and formation of bones and muscles and for full nerve functioning. Calcium, in the form of chalk, was first added to bread during the war as a way of compensating for the fail in availability of dairy foods. Nowadays, the addition is of little value. Recommended levels of calcium intake are met in abundance through the rest of our diet, without the consumption of bread at all.

Vitamins B1, B2 and Niacin

These vitamins are part of the vitamin B complex (of which there are 12) and are necessary for the utilisation of carbohydrate and for the proper functioning of the nervous system, so are a fairly beneficial addition. But so are all the other vitamins in the B complex, for the full benefit of which all are needed together, not separately. So although the addition of these three vitamins is welcome, it would be even more so if the other B vitamins were also added, (or, some would rather say, not removed in the first place!).

And what of all the other vitamins and minerals removed during the refining process? Vitamin E, for example, is found mainly in the germ of the grain and is completely destroyed when the grain is refined. Necessary for the formation of tissues and for the reproductive system, Vitamin E is an essential vitamin, not found in many other foods. And it is not replaced in white flour.

Apart from the high nutritional loss in the making of white flour, there is also the loss of the bran, the outer layer of the grain. Bran is now sold as a separate product or food supplement and there is no doubt that for many long-term sufferers of constipation, it has proved to be a God-send! Basically, the greater the fibre (bran is largely fibre) content in our diet, the more easily and quickly will food pass through our digestive system and the less likely it is to get blocked on route. This is because fibre is so constructed that the body cannot fully break it down, we can absorb the nutrients but it passes through our body only partly digested. This means that in the intestines there is more bulk which is also fairly moist having absorbed plenty of water. On a highly refined diet, with little or no fibre, food has been found to stay in the body, in the digestive system, for up to 100 hours, thereby moving through the body very slowly. On a diet containing natural, unrefined foods, with plenty of fibre, the food can pass through the body in only 36 hours and puts far less strain on the muscles in the intestines.

There are now a number of illnesses on the increase that can be directly related to a highly refined diet, especially one lacking in fibre. Diverticulotis is one, where the walls of the intestines rupture and the small ruptures or sacs can cause acute inflammation and pain. It is an illness only found to any great extent in countries where refined foods are eaten, as one of the main causes is the pressure on the intestinal walls caused by these foods. Cancer of the intestines is another such illness, now very much on the increase and one of the main reasons is felt to be the long time refined foods take to pass through the body. Other illnesses attributed to a high consumption of refined carbohydrates are: appendicitis, varicose veins, ulcers, haemorrhoids and even heart disease. However, if one is eating wholewheat products, there should be no need to add extra bran to one's diet at all. It is a food supplement, especially needed by those suffering from the result of a refined diet.

As we have seen, bread has always been the staple food for man. Wholewheat bread, or bread made from any other whole grain flour, can justifiably stand up to the claim of being 'the staff of life', as it contains protein, unsaturated fat, 24 vitamins and minerals and carbohydrate — in other words, it is a complete and necessary food containing nearly all we need to sustain life. Can white bread be said to fulfill the same qualities? Bread is as much a staple food now as it ever was in the past but nutritionally it does not compare. Little wonder then, as we are still eating so much of it, that we are also suffering from the effect of it. Possibly one of the main difficulties lies in the lack of understanding and knowledge that the average consumer has about nutrition. The qualities looked for in a loaf of bread (or any food for that matter) are freshness, appearance and taste, as if these qualities in themselves denote high nutrition. The fact that the product may contain no real nutritional value at all does not occur, it is not even thought of. As long as it looks good then it must do us good, no connection between what we eat and our state of health is made.

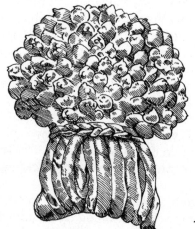

TRADITIONAL HARVEST LOAF

Chapter III

Flour and Other Bread Making Ingredients

Before going any further, it is necessary to describe 'gluten', as it is mentioned a number of times in this chapter. Gluten is made up of various proteins which form the skin of thousands of tiny balloons. These balloons, or bubbles, hold the gas produced by the growing yeast (or rising agent) in the bread. Without these balloons the gas would simply escape and the bread would not rise. So flour high in gluten makes for a well-risen loaf.

Wheat

Wheat flour is the most commonly used flour for bread, with most manufactured bread being made from hard Canadian wheat. Hard, or strong, wheat is that which is grown in a hot, sunny climate with a low rainfall, a climate which raises the gluten level in the wheat, therefore the flour makes a lighter loaf. Weak, or soft wheat, is that grown in a climate low in sunshine but high in rain, which creates a low gluten level and therefore a smaller, denser loaf. Soft wheat is grown in Britain whereas the wheat grown in Canada and the USA is ideal hard wheat. Most bakers claim that the customer would not want a loaf made with British wheat as it is heavier, but British wheat can be used successfully by the home-baker, so long as it is recognised that it may not rise quite so well. Some people complain that wholewheat bread is too heavy, but maybe it is just a matter of what we are used to, what we have been conditioned to like. Others complain that white bread is too light! Even home-made bread that hasn't risen much and seems a bit stodgy, is still a far fuller and satisfying bread than any commercial bread.

There are a number of advantages for using local or home-grown wheat, even if it is a soft wheat, as opposed to using imported wheat. Firstly, imported wheat, even if the flour is stoneground, is often not organically grown, i.e. it will have been sprayed with chemical insecticides or pesticides, whereas it is fairly easy to obtain organically grown local wheat. Secondly, by using wheat grown in one's own country, we are using a food that has grown in the same climate as ourselves, rather than a completely different one. Thirdly, it is a way of helping to keep down the amount of food imported into one's country and in turn helps support local farmers. Quite a few of the most common brand names of wholewheat flour in Britain use imported Canadian wheat, as it does make a better loaf. But local wheat is easily available and can sometimes even be bought direct from the farmer.

Wheat flour is milled to different extraction rates:

100% — here the whole of the grain is milled, with nothing removed.

85% — here the bran (15%) has been sifted out of the flour, making it slightly lighter, but with less fibre. Rather than buying these two different types of flour separately, it is more economical to buy just 100% and then sieve it oneself to extract the 15% bran if a lighter flour is required. The bran can then be used in other dishes.

81% — This flour has had 19% sieved out, making it a lighter flour still but it does mean it has lost more of its nutritional value. 81% and 85% are sometimes called wheatmeal flour, but this can also be ordinary white flour with some bran put back in.

70–76% — This flour has had the bran and the germ completely removed, before the milling, to make white flour.

Unbleached white flour — It is possible to buy this flour, that is approximately 75% extraction but with no added bleaches or chemicals. It is no more nutritious than ordinary white flour but possibly safer due to the lack of additives.

Strong white flour — Usually recommended for making white bread as this is
the strong Canadian flour, as opposed to the ordinary soft white cake or
biscuit English flour.

All flours are at their best when freshly milled, but wholewheat will go
rancid after 4–6 months. It is still safe to use it after this time but it will have a
slightly sour taste. The whole grain will, however, keep indefinitely if kept dry
and cool and not milled into flour.

Wholewheat grain (cooked) is a nice addition to bread, giving it added
texture. Broken wheat is added to granary bread to give it its crunch. Wheat
flakes can also be added.

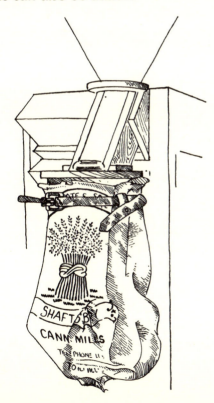

Rye

Rye was known as the 'poor man's wheat' for a very long time although it has now nearly died out in Britain, with only Russian, Polish or German cookery still really favouring it. Rye has a wonderful taste but if used on its own will produce a rather heavy, flat bread for although it has a fairly high gluten content, it does not have the same structure as wheat and is unable to hold the gas when rising. It is easiest to make if mixed with approximately 50% wheat flour.

Rye bread is especially good made with a sour dough recipe as this enhances the naturally slightly sour taste of rye. It is possible to buy organic rye flour or grain from which to make one's own flour.

Barley

Barley was also one of the main bread flours of the past, as well as being the staple food of Tibet where a mixture of barley flour, tea and butter was made into rolls and cooked over open fires. As a flour for bread it is low in gluten, so is best mixed with wheat flour to help it rise. It has a very special flavour and is particularly good with lots of herbs as a savoury loaf. It is also good for making sauces and crumble toppings, and it is from barley that we make malt.

Oats

Oatmeal (available as coarse, medium and fine) or oat flour (finer than fine oatmeal) is very low in gluten so produces a flat, heavy bread on its own. But either oatmeal or oat flakes added to bread can give it a lovely chewy and light texture. Oats are high in protein but also fairly high in essential fats which means that they tend to go rancid fairly quickly, unless stored as the whole grain, groats.

Corn

Called either corn or maize and available as both meal and flour, which can be a bit confusing! The meal is a bit coarser than the flour, both a lovely rich yellow colour. Commercial white cornflour is made from the refined grain and has little nutritional value, whilst the yellow cornflour is made from the whole grain.

Corn is very underused in Britain, but is grown and used considerably in South America and in Italy for a staple dish called 'Polenta'. Low in gluten, corn bread is a flat yellow bread with a rich flavour. Used with wheat it makes a lovely golden loaf, with a good texture or use it for making sauces, crumble toppings etc.

It is worth noting here that arrowroot powder (made from the dried roots of the arrowroot plant) works in a similar way to commercial cornflour, in making a thick clear sauce, but it is far more nutritious. It is used in exactly the same way.

Rice
Brown rice flour (not to be confused with ordinary white rice flour or ground rice) is very low in gluten and not that suitable for bread making, being a very dense, moist flour, although small quantities can be mixed with wheat flour. It is, however, ideal for sauces, sweet dishes, biscuits and makes a lovely creamy pudding when cooked, like semolina, with milk and honey. This is especially loved by babies!

Cooked whole rice is a useful addition to bread, adding extra texture and helping to keep the bread moist for longer.

Buckwheat
Buckwheat has a highly distinctive taste but like rice it is low in gluten and makes a very dense bread on its own. As a bread, when made with wheat flour, it is dark and close textured, but with a lovely rich flavour. It is ideal for pancakes, especially savoury ones, muffins and waffles. Cooked buckwheat is also good added to bread — approximately one cup per pound of flour.

Millet
Millet flour is hard to come by and when made into bread makes a very flat, soft loaf. When mixed with wheat flour, a much better loaf is produced but the millet flavour can be lost. Millet flakes added to bread give extra lightness

or they can be cooked with a little water and made into a thick savoury cream, with seasonings.

Soya
Soya flour can be used as a nutritious addition to bread and cakes, whilst not altering the texture too much. It adds a lot of extra protein but is very rich and it is not advisable to use too much at once. Approximately 3–4 oz soya flour per pound of wheat flour is plenty.

Bean flours
Flours such as chick pea or lentil (Gram) have come to us from the East where they are mainly used for making into flat breads like chappatis, or for making batters into which vegetables are dipped before being fried.

Other Ingredients
Other ingredients in bread can be numerous, the American loaf has been known to have up to 93 added ingredients! Home-made bread has one great advantage — at least you know what has gone into it.

Yeast
Wild yeasts are all around us — the bloom on plums and grapes, on berries, leaves and bark, are all natural yeasts. Yeast is also present in fermented liquor, the yeast on the grape being a natural fermentation agent. The use of yeast for bread was probably first discovered when liquor or beer found its way into some dough. Previous to the use of yeast as a rising agent was the use of small amounts of fermented bread dough (see sour dough bread) which had been fermenting for a few days. Breads made with yeast are leavened, unleavened breads being much heavier and flatter.

Over the years it has been discovered that yeast is a single cell plant and when given the right conditions — warmth and moisture — these cells will multiply rapidly. As they do this they convert the starch into sugar, releasing carbon dioxide (gas) which, in trying to find a way out, lifts and aerates the dough. This is where the gluten in the flour is so important as it allows the dough to expand without allowing the gas to escape. When the bread is cooked, this gas is destroyed but the bread remains risen.

To grow happily the yeast needs certain foods as well as warmth and moisture. Best of all it likes sugar. But this does not mean that one has to administer large doses of white sugar, since too much sugar will kill the yeast. Instead it prefers the natural weaker sugars found in honey or malt extract. It also gets what it needs from the starch contained in the flour. Only if using dried yeast is any form of extra sweetening needed and here it needs only to be a teaspoon of honey, while fresh yeast does not need anything added as the warmth of the water is sufficient to start it activating.

Fresh yeast, looking somewhat like putty if kept dry and cool, as in a fridge or cool larder, will keep alive but dormant for up to 3 weeks before it begins to die. When it does this it goes a darker colour and smells stronger. It can be deep frozen for up to 3 months. The dried yeast granules, which will last for up to 3 years if kept really air-tight, are air-dried, which leaves the yeast cells dormant.

As yeast has such remarkable growing powers, the longer one is able to leave the dough to rise, the less yeast will be needed initially: 1 oz of fresh yeast being enough for 3 lbs of flour if left for 2–3 hours, but only ½ oz would be needed if it was left for 7–8 hours. When leaving bread to rise for a long time, however, do punch it down and knead it for a few minutes every hour or so. Otherwise the yeast can die in the gas it produces. Kneading the bread releases the gas and introduces fresh oxygen. When using dried yeast, only half the amount of yeast is needed to the amount of fresh yeast as it is more active. Fresh yeast need only be dissolved in a little warm water before being used, whilst dried yeast needs to be left for 10 minutes or so in warm water with a little honey or malt to activate and froth up.

Sour Dough

Before yeast was discovered as a rising agent, it was common practice to leave a small amount of dough for a few days, during which time it soured slightly, and then to mix this into the main bread dough, as it helped it to rise. This type of bread has come to be called sour dough, due to its slightly sour taste. The rising agent is called a starter. It is easily made and the fermented properties of the starter are very beneficial to the digestive system, stimulating the enzymes. The bread produced has a slightly sour taste, which most people find very pleasant and the bread often rises very well. See recipe section for details on how to make a starter. Starters have been known to last for years, as out of each batch of bread dough, one takes a fresh starter to replenish the old. In some parts of the world (i.e. Germany and America) this is a very popular method for making bread, pancakes and muffins.

Oatcakes were traditionally made in this way too. The baker would use the same bowl for making his oatcake batter in, leaving a little in the bottom each time. No rising agent was needed as the sour dough quality helped the cakes to rise.

Cream of Tartar

Cream of tartar and bicarbonate of soda were the two main ingredients in commercial baking powder. Cream of tartar is especially interesting as, like yeast and the sour dough starter, it is a naturally fermented rising agent. When wine is made in wooden wine vats and then poured out, there remains a white sediment on the inside of the vat. Scraped off and dried, this is cream of tartar. Unfortunately, most wine merchants now use metal wine vats and this same process does not occur, so cream of tartar is becoming harder to obtain. Look closely at tins of baking powder now on sale and more than likely you will see that the ingredients are: Bicarbonate of soda, acid sodium pyrophosphate and acid calcium phosphate, chemical replacements for cream of tartar. It is, though, still available as a separate product. Apart from these chemical replacements, bicarb of soda is known to have detrimental effects on vitamin B when used in baking, so can cancel out one of the main advantages of using wholewheat flour.

Baking powder in cakes can be omitted altogether and replaced with just cream of tartar; or try creaming a little (¼ oz) fresh yeast in at the beginning of making the cake, then leave the mixture to rise for a few minutes prior to baking; or beat the whites of any eggs used separately and fold them in at the end of the mixing process. Alternatively, omit all rising agents altogether and just let the cake be as it is — slightly heavier and a little more solid than you may be used to but just as tasty.

Sugar, Honey, Molasses and Malt

Sugar is not a necessary ingredient in bread as so many bread recipes would have us believe — in fact it can have a detrimental effect. It is an extremely concentrated unnatural form of sucrose, found nowhere in nature in such strength. It can be omitted from cakes and biscuits just as easily as it can from bread and replaced with either honey or a mixture of honey, malt or molasses. If sugar is to be used (as in some biscuit recipes) then the heavy moist molasses or muscavado sugar should be used as this is slightly less concentrated and does contain some nutritional value, as opposed to white sugar, which contains no nutritional value whatsoever.

Molasses is extracted as sugar is refined and it contains valuable nutrients such as iron and vitamin B. Black treacle is similar to molasses but contains a higher content of sugar. Molasses used in cooking adds a rich flavour, sweetness and a lovely dark colour, but it does have quite a strong taste so do not overdo it if you are not used to it.

Honey also contains sucrose — but in a natural and far less concentrated form which the body is able to digest more easily and which does not have the same harmful effects. Sucrose itself is not harmful, unless it is taken in very concentrated and large amounts, as in white sugar. Honey also contains many other beneficial nutrients. If using it in cake recipes instead of sugar, then simply reduce the liquid content in the recipe slightly.

Malt extract can also be used instead of sugar for making bread and mixed with honey for cakes. Like honey, malt also contains sucrose, but in a natural form as is found in all whole grains. Malt is made from sprouted and slightly fermented barley, so is a very natural product and is rich in vitamin B, iron and other trace minerals.

Salt

Most people prefer salt in their bread, but it is very much a matter of choice and certainly not essential. It does tend to slow down the rising effect of yeast slightly, so if large amounts of salt are added, extra time will be needed for the bread to rise.

Pure sea or rock salt will be found to have a fuller taste as well as being rich in minerals and free of the chemicals added to commercial salt.

Oil

Most ordinary bread recipes call for the addition of 1–2 oz fat, either butter, oil or lard. It is a very small amount and can be omitted completely without making that much difference. Its main use is in helping to keep the bread fresh. Butter will make an especially rich crust which can be nice but there is no need for lard (animal fat) to be used at any time. Oil used in bread (approximately 3 tbs per 3 lbs of flour) adds workability to the dough and improves the texture, as well as enriching the crust.

Eggs

Eggs are not normally added to ordinary bread recipes but used in special bread and cake recipes. They add texture, lightness and help the ingredients bind together where no yeast has been used. Egg whites, whipped and folded in separately, will help the mixture to rise.

Water

Water in bread is obviously necessary, although milk can be used instead. What is most important is the temperature of the water. Too hot and it will kill the yeast, too cool and the yeast will take longer to activate. Best of all is a temperature between 98°F – 108°F, but a thermometer is not essential, experience of 'hand-hot' being more important. Blood temperature is what to aim at so when testing with your finger, it should be neither too hot nor too cold, but nicely warm.

Flour absorbs different amounts of water so it is always difficult to give exact quantities. The flour you use may need more or less water than stated in the recipe so adjust accordingly. If you are concerned at all about the chemicals being added to your water supply, then simple water filters are available through major wholefood shops that are very effective. Alternatively, use water that has been boiled and cooled.

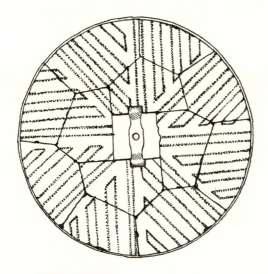

MILL-STONE

Chapter IV

How To Make It

How to make bread? There are dozens of recipes available in nearly every cookbook ever written, although what tends to happen is that each cook develops in their own way the method best suited to them. The different methods vary mainly in the number of risings the dough has before baking; basically the more risings, the higher the bread will be, as it gives the yeast more time to develop, but one can make successful loaves with only one quick rising and no kneading at all. The thing to do is to try out the different methods and see which you prefer. Many people are put off bread making by thinking it all takes so long to do, so maybe start with the 'Quick Make' method and discover the bread you can make from start to finish in little over an hour. And remember — although bread risen say 3 times, over a long period, might seem to take ages to make, it doesn't mean that you have to be with it all the time. The amount of time you actually spend with the bread may be very little and you can get on with other things in the meantime. Bread making is really very simple and it is possible to get good results every time you make it — there are no hidden secrets!

Always allow the loaves to cool before you cut them, as hot dough can cause upset stomachs and the loaf is likely to collapse.

Things that can go wrong
There are a few things that can go wrong, but an understanding of them can only lead to better bread, so do not despair if your first baking efforts fail!

Bread failing to rise: Here either the water was too hot and thereby killed the yeast or the warm place where the dough was left to rise was too hot. Alternatively the flour used was naturally low in gluten, like English wheat, rye or barley flour, so would not rise much anyway. Extra kneading will help.

Crust comes apart: Here the bread may have risen too quickly which can happen if the warm place is too warm; or the dough wasn't kneaded or mixed enough, causing the yeast to be distributed unevenly or air to be trapped inside.

Bread dry and heavy: Either not enough water content in the dough, so making it a bit dry, or the bread was cooked for too long, drying out in the oven. If this is the case, turn the oven up a little and cook for a shorter length of time. Remember too, that extra flour can be added to a wet dough, but it is much more difficult to add extra water to a dry dough.

Bread uncooked in the middle: Here either the bread was cooked too quickly, thereby cooking on the outside but not in the middle, so try reducing the temperature of your oven and cooking for a little longer; or the dough was too moist, like rye which can be a bit sticky. Add a little extra wheat flour to help this.

Bread rises and sinks again: This is mainly due to a low gluten level in the flour. It is able to hold the gas initially as the bread rises but if it is knocked or moved slightly, the gas escapes and the bread sinks. One answer is to leave the bread to rise for the last time in the oven, so that it isn't moved again before being baked, but this is not ideal as it does not allow for the oven to be heated prior to baking. Kneading the dough more will help as this develops the gluten level, also allowing the dough to rise slowly, then moving it carefully.

Crust sticks to tins: If the bread isn't coming out of the tins easily and maybe even leaving the crust behind, then allow the loaves to cool in the tins for five minutes before easing them out with a knife. This is usually caused by tins that have not been seasoned fully (see Equipment, below); a wet dough, in which case dust the tins with flour after oiling them; or the loaf may not be fully cooked, so return it to the oven for another 5–10 minutes.

Equipment

To make bread you will need a big bowl. A china (earthenware) one is best if possible. A measuring jug is useful but a clean milk bottle will measure a pint or ½ pint if you are careful. Scales are very handy, especially as cup measurements can easily go wrong if you use a different sized cup to the one in the recipe. A big wooden spoon is essential as is also a nice place to knead the dough. Most people prefer wood, marble is good but can make the dough a bit chilly; really all that is important is a working top of the right height, with an easy-to-clean surface.

Good bread tins are important but that doesn't necessarily mean brand new ones. The best type are the cheap aluminium ones once they have been well sealed with oil and usage. When new, the bread tends to stick to these pans and they can have a slightly metal taste. To seal them, coat them in oil

EQUIPMENT

on the inside and bake for 10 minutes in a hot oven. Repeat a few times, without washing in between. After baking bread also avoid washing the tins, just wipe clean with a cloth or, if washing is necessary, avoid scouring or using washing-up liquids as the soap will break down the non-stick surface you have made and you will find your bread sticking again. The non-stick tins are a temptation as they are easy to use but once the non-stick coating begins to scratch, then it can become toxic. Also they tend to come in a long, low shape, whereas the aluminium ones come in a slightly shorter, but higher shaped, tin which makes a higher loaf as the sides of the tin help to support the dough as it is rising. Earthenware flower pots can also be used to make bread (4–6″) but do seal them well with oil first, as for the aluminium pans above, since they are very porous and will stick easily.

For rolls or round loaves, a flat baking tray is all that is needed, although round loaves (like cobs) can also be done in cake tins. Special round bread tins are available in some good shops.

The old fashioned tart trays with patterns in the bottom of each tart container make nice holders for rolls as you end up with each roll having a pattern on its bottom. And finally, a jar with oil in it and a small (¼″) paintbrush is the easiest way to oil your tins.

Kneading
Kneading is essential as it not only mixes the dough but it also releases the gas produced by the growing yeast and gives it fresh oxygen to continue growing. Otherwise it can get too gassy and the yeast may die — it needs oxygen to grow happily. So kneading helps the yeast to grow fully as well as improving the texture of the dough. In the 'Quick Make' method the kneading is replaced with a thorough mixing but as the bread has only one rising before being baked, there is little chance of the yeast gassing itself. Kneading also helps the bread to rise more as it develops the strength and structure of the gluten.

Everyone has their own way of kneading but essentially it is a matter of using the fists and punching the dough out flat, then folding it back upon itself, before punching it out again. Experiment and find your own method. If you have done pottery then treat the dough as you would clay. Above all be firm and confident. Knead for a good five minutes or until the dough becomes smooth and elastic. As you get used to kneading you will find that the dough tells you when it is ready.

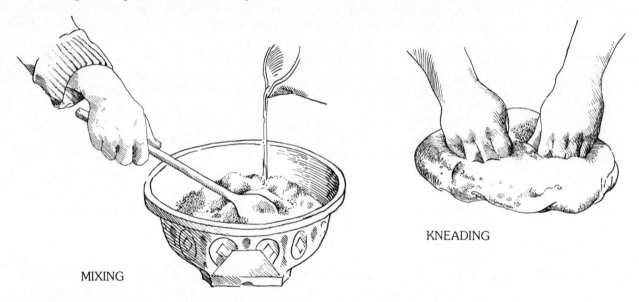

KNEADING

MIXING

A warm place

In all bread recipes one finds the need for a warm place in which to put the dough to rise. A warm place is only necessary if you wish the dough to rise within an hour, whereas if you want to leave it to rise more slowly, then leave it at room temperature. If you want to leave it all day then put it in a cool place (larder or fridge), it will still rise but very much more slowly.

A warm place will be whatever you have — an airing cupboard, next to a water heater, above an Aga, or put the oven on low for a few minutes, put the bowl in and turn the oven off, it will stay nice and warm for quite a while.

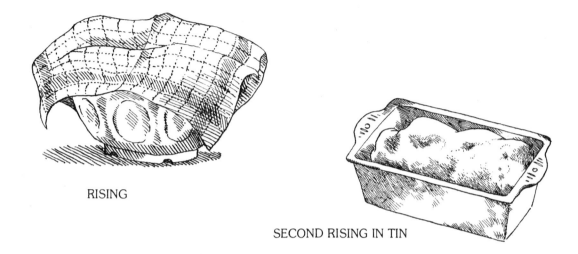

RISING

SECOND RISING IN TIN

Covering the bowl with a cloth helps to keep it warm. Putting it in a polythene bag also helps to keep it warm and is advantageous if you are going out and leaving the bread to rise without supervision — if by any chance it rises too much then you won't have dough everywhere to greet you on your return. The only warning is not to leave it in too hot a place or the yeast will quickly die.

BAKED LOAF

Bread Shapes

Tin: This is a loaf made in an oblong tin. Knead bread and form into an oblong. Drop into the tin, filling it half full and press down lightly. For a patterned top, slit with a knife about ½″ deep across the loaf.

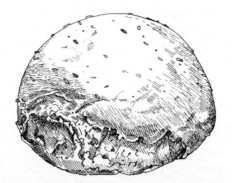

Cob: A round loaf (traditionally granary) baked either on a flat baking sheet or in a round bread or cake tin. Form dough into a round and place on flat sheet, then tuck the edges underneath all round, towards the centre, so it ends up looking like a puffed-up cushion. This will stop the dough from spreading as it rises and will keep it round.

Cottage: Like a cob but with a smaller round on top. Divide the dough into two, but with one part bigger than the other. Form both into rounds as above and place the smaller one on top. Then make a hole through the middle of both with the handle of a wooden spoon dipped in flour.

Bloomer: Long, baton shaped loaf with slashes along the top, traditionally for rye bread. Knead dough and form into oval-oblong shape. Tuck edges underneath as for cob and then slash the top diagonally with a knife.

Plait: This can be done in a number of different ways, with any number of
   strands. Here are two fairly easy ways:
  1. Divide one pound of dough into three equal parts. Roll each part into a
      long sausage. Lay them side by side and, starting from the middle,
      working towards you, plait them together, pinching the ends. Then turn
      the plait over and plait again from the middle to the end. Seal ends and
      put the plait on a flat baking tray to rise.
  2. Roll one pound of dough into an oblong. Divide into three lengthways
      by marking but not cutting. Here it is nice if a fruit filling is spread down
      the middle section. Cut the two outside oblong sections into diagonal
      strips then fold them alternately over the middle. Seal edges and brush
      with egg.
Rolls: Divide dough into small pieces. Form into rounds as for cob, tucking
   the edges underneath on a flat tray.
Crown: Put five rolls close together on the baking tray, with one in the
   middle. They will fuse together as they rise and can then be pulled apart
   to form individual rolls when cooked.

Topping the Loaf

To improve the look and finished texture of your loaf, various toppings are suggested with the recipes:

Brush with:
1.   Water, for a crisp crust.
2.   Oil, for an extra crunchy crust.
3.   Milk, for a softer finish (i.e. for rolls).
4.   Egg yolk and milk mixed for a glossy, golden finish.
5.   Warmed milk and honey for sweet tea breads.
6.   Just honey, added near the end of baking, for a sticky top.
7.   Sprinkle with poppy, caraway or sesame seeds or with crushed wheat for an extra tasting, crunchy topping.

Apply these toppings either before baking or ten minutes before the end of baking, or both.

Oven Temperatures

Each of the following recipes has an oven temperature for gas and °F. Below is a guide for the conversion to °C and for solid fuel cookers. Ovens vary considerably, so you may need to adjust accordingly. Often new ovens are much hotter than old ones.

gas	°F	°C	solid fuel
1	275	140	very slow
2	300	150	medium
3	325	160	medium
4	350	180	medium
5	375	190	fairly hot
6	400	205	hot
7	425	220	hot
8	450	230	very hot
9	475	240	very hot

Metric Conversion

As all the recipes are in pounds and ounces, here is a conversion table to grams and litres.

1 oz — 29 gm

2 oz — 58 gm

4 oz — 115 gm

8 oz — 230 gm

12 oz — 345 gm

1 lb — 460 gm

2.2 lb — 1 kg

9 fl oz — 250 ml (¼ lt)

18 fl oz — 500 ml (½ lt)

1¾ pint — 1 litre

British-American Conversion

tbs — level British tablespoon or heaped American tablespoon

dsp — level British dessertspoon or heaped American dessertspoon

tsp — level British teaspoon or heaped American teaspoon

1 pint = British pint (20 fl oz) or 1¼ American pints (16 fl oz + 4 fl oz)

½ pint = 10 fl oz

¼ pint = 5 fl oz

⅓ pint = approx 7 fl oz

Chapter V

How To Bake It Recipes

Here are six basic methods for making bread, followed by lots of variations and then more specialised recipes.

Please note that in all the recipes, whenever flour or wheat flour is mentioned, 100% should be used. 85% or white flour are not used in any of the recipes. When using honey, it is easiest if runny honey is used, or melted thick honey.

One Rising or Quick Make Bread

This is a foolproof recipe, very easy to make, with no kneading! The bread produced is fairly moist, with a more spongy type texture, which keeps well.

Warnings: being a moist dough, it does not hold its own shape when rising as ordinary dough does and once it reaches the top of the tins it starts to flop over the sides, so keep an eye on it. If it does go over the sides, then push back and leave to rise to the top again. You don't get a nicely rounded loaf with this method, it tends to be rather flat on top. Also, being fairly moist, it can easily stick to the sides of the tins so make sure they are well oiled. If using fairly new tins then after oiling, dust lightly with flour.

For 2 loaves (using 2 lbs flour)

2 lbs flour (100% or a mixture of other flours)
1 oz fresh yeast or
½ oz dried yeast and 1 tsp honey
2 tsp salt
1 pint and a little extra warm water

Dissolve the yeast in ½ pint of warm water, adding the honey and leaving to froth for 10 minutes if using dried yeast. Mix the salt into the flour and any oil required, plus any extra ingredients (see ideas below). Add the yeast and a further ½ pint of warm water and mix really well. Now add a little extra warm water (approx. 1–3 fl oz). Different flours will require different amounts, but one is aiming to achieve a dough that is too moist to knead with the hands but is just moist enough to be able to beat with a spoon, not so it is actually wet. Again, experiment, after a couple of tries you will soon learn how much is needed. Beat really well then divide and put into two well oiled tins and leave to rise in a warm place, putting them in the oven just as the dough comes to the tops of the tins. Bake for 15 mins, 400°F, reg. 6, then for 25 mins at 375°F, reg. 5. Take the bread out of the tins and put them back in the oven, upside down, for 5 mins, to get a good crust all over. Baking them in this way helps the moist dough to cook all through.

For one loaf, use only half the quantities.

Two Risings or Ordinary Bread

This is the sort of recipe most commonly found in recipe books or on flour packets. It makes a good, easy to cut and firm loaf.

For 2 loaves (using 2 lb tins)

2 lbs flour
1 oz fresh yeast or
½ oz dried yeast and 1 tsp honey
2 tsp salt
2 tbs oil (optional)
1 pint warm water
extra flour for kneading

Dissolve the yeast in ½ pint warm water, adding the honey and leaving for 10 minutes if using dried yeast. Mix the salt and the oil with the flour and any other extra ingredients. Then mix the yeast into the flour with a further ¼ pint warm water. Mix well, adding the further ¼ pint warm water as required to make a firm but soft dough.

Turn out onto a floured work top and knead for a few minutes. If your bowl is big enough then one can knead the dough inside the bowl instead. Add any extra flour as you knead if the dough is a bit sticky, or a little extra water if the dough is a bit dry. Put the dough back in the bowl and cover with a warm cloth. Leave to rise in a warm place until doubled in size (about 30–45 minutes).

Tip the dough out onto your board and knead again for a few minutes. Divide into two and shape into loaves, then press down into the bread tins. Leave to rise again in a warm place until the dough fills the tins. Bake at 400°F, reg. 6 for 35 minutes, then take the loaves out of the tins and return to the oven upside down for a further few minutes, turning the oven down to 350°F, reg. 4. Cool.

Three Risings or Slow Bread

This method uses exactly the same ingredients as the last method, 'Ordinary' bread, and the method is the same up until the dough has doubled in size for the first time. Then knead the dough well again for a few minutes, put back in the bowl and leave to rise again in a warm place. After this second rising, the bread is kneaded again before being put in the tins and left to rise for a third time. It makes a slightly lighter loaf, of a very fine texture and well risen as the yeast has had more time to grow.

Three Risings or Batter Bread

This method starts with a batter, leaving that to rise first. This produces a very fine loaf indeed, so is well worth trying.

For 2 loaves (using 2 lb tins)

2 lbs flour
1 oz fresh yeast or
½ oz dried yeast and 1 tsp honey
2 tsp salt
2 tbs oil
1¼ pints warm water
extra flour for kneading

Dissolve the yeast in the ¼ pint warm water, adding the honey if using dried yeast. Meanwhile put 1 lb of your flour in a bowl, add the yeast and the further 1 pint of warm water. Beat really well into a thick batter. Leave to double in size in a warm place.

When risen, add 2 tsp salt, the oil and any extra ingredients you may like to add plus your second pound of flour. Turn onto a floured board and knead for a few minutes, adding extra flour if the dough is a bit sticky. Put back into the bowl and leave to rise again till double in size.

Knead the dough again for a few minutes then divide in two, press into the tins and leave to rise again before baking. Bake at 400°F, reg. 6 for 35 mins, then remove from the tins and return to the oven for 5 mins, at 350°F, reg. 4. Cool.

Unleavened Bread

Unleavened bread has no rising agents at all so makes a heavier, chewier bread, with a really full taste. It can be made with any mixture of flours and with added whole grains (cooked), nuts, fruit, vegetables, etc. It will rise a little if left overnight in a warm place before baking.

The recipe

There isn't one! All you need to do is mix your flour with warm water until you have a thick batter. Leave overnight or for a few hours in a warm place. In the morning mix in a little salt, any other ingredients you fancy and enough flour to form a dough. Knead well, divide and put into two tins.

Leave in a warm place for 1–2 hours, when the loaves will rise a little. Then bake at 375°F, reg. 5 for 35-40 mins.

Sour Dough

Sour dough bread is made with a naturally fermented rising agent, called a starter, and the resulting bread has a slightly sour but very pleasing taste. The fermented food that the starter is made from forms enzymes that are very good for the digestive system.

To make a starter:

The simplest method is to mix together 4 tbs flour with 4-5 tbs water (enough of each to form a thick batter) and put in a jar or bowl, not filling the jar to the top but leaving some air space. Any left-over cooked grains, beans, vegetables, bread dough or pastry can also be added. Leave the starter to ferment for 4–6 days, shaking the jar occasionally. It will activate a bit quicker in a warm place. When it smells really sour and is getting bubbly, then it is ready. This is your starter and can be replenished with each batch of bread, when it should be left again for a few days before being used. Any cooked food can be added to it, yogurt or even yeast, and potato water is traditionally used as it ferments quickly. If your starter starts to get too strong then leave it in the fridge, which will slow down the fermentation. Starters can go on indefinitely, treat them with care and they will never let you down. The older they are, the better they will rise. If you keep the starter in the fridge then just add left-overs to it as you go along and take a jam jar out for your bread each baking day.

For 2 loaves (using 2 lb tins)

1 jam jar of starter
2 lb flour
2 tsp salt
2 tbs oil
approx. ¾ pint warm water

At night, mix together 1 lb of flour and the starter with the water. Beat really well, then cover and leave overnight in a warm place.

In the morning remove 1 cup of the batter to replenish your starter. Then add the salt, oil and remaining pound of flour plus any extras you fancy. Mix well, adding a little extra flour or water if needed to form a good dough. Knead for a few minutes then divide and put into two tins. Slit the tops with a knife and then leave to rise in a warm place for 1–2 hours. Bake for 35 mins, 400°F, reg. 6. Remove the loaves from the tins and return to the oven for 5 mins., 350°F, reg. 4.

Warning: sour dough is very temperamental and you may find that even after 2 hours it still hasn't risen. Do not despair. Bake anyway and be surprised – invariably it rises in the oven; other times it will rise beautifully before baking. You can never tell.

QUERN

Sesame Bread

Add 1 tbs sesame seeds to any 1 lb of flour in any of the above recipes. Use sesame oil in the recipe too and then roll the loaves in sesame seeds before putting them in the tins. Either roasted or unroasted sesame seeds can be used, the roasted ones giving a slightly stronger flavour.

Poppy Bread

Add 1 tbs poppy seeds to any 1 lb of flour in the above recipes, especially good with rye bread. Brush the tops of the loaves with milk or beaten egg and sprinkle with poppy seeds before baking.

Caraway Bread

Add 1 tbs caraway seeds per 1 lb of flour in any of the above recipes. Brush the loaves with milk and sprinkle with caraway seeds before baking. Especially good with rye or buckwheat loaves. Caraway seeds have been called 'little moments of sudden awareness' – try them and see.

Sunflower Bread

Add 2 oz chopped, ground or roasted sunflower seeds to any 1 lb of flour in the above recipes, then brush the tops of the loaves with milk and sprinkle with whole seeds before baking. Try adding 1 tbs tamari soya sauce to the dough as well, for a slightly savoury loaf.

Herb Bread

Add either 3 tsp dried or 2 tbs fresh herbs per 1 lb of flour. Use whatever you fancy – thyme, oregano and chives are nice but most people seem to find their own favourites. Try adding 1–2 tbs tamari soya sauce to the dough as well, to make it more savoury. A slice of herby bread is a lovely accompaniment to a salad or soup.

Sprouted Bread

Sprouted wheat, alfalfa, green lentils or aduki beans go really well in bread (as do any sprouts – mung, sunflower, fenugreek etc.). Mix in a cupful or two of the raw sprouts into the flour before making into a dough. Adds taste, texture and nutrition. Fenugreek makes a spicy bread, sunflower is nutty whilst aduki and alfalfa are sweet and crunchy.

Simple Fruit Bread

To every 1 lb of flour, add 4 oz raisins, sultanas or chopped dates (or all three) and 1 tbs honey or malt extract. If the fruit is soaked first it will make a moister bread that keeps well. Brush with egg and honey.

Apricot Bread

Add 4 oz apricots stewed in the juice of 1 lemon and 2 tbs honey. Slightly less water may be needed to make a firm dough. Brush with egg and honey.

Nut Bread

To every 1 lb of flour, add 4 oz chopped nuts (try hazels or walnuts). Brush the loaf with egg and honey and arrange a few nuts on top.

Fruit and Nut Bread

To every 1 lb of flour, add 1 tsp cinnamon, 3 oz chopped nuts, 3 oz dried fruit and 1 tbs honey. Brush with milk and honey.

Whole Grain Bread

Cooked whole grain, like rice, buckwheat or wheat makes a bread chewier, moister, very satisfying and helps keep the bread moist for longer. Add 1 or 2 cups cooked grain to the flour before making into a dough. You may find it more difficult to knead as it will be softer and more crumbly than usual.

Buckwheat Bread

A dark, close textured and full tasting loaf. Add 4 oz buckwheat flour to any 1 lb of wheat flour in the above recipes. Too much buckwheat flour used at once will make the loaf rather heavy and sticky, although a proportion of 50% buckwheat flour to 50% wheat flour will work.

Oat Bread

Oats, either as meal or flakes, make a lovely addition to bread, adding texture and taste. They can be added to any of the bread methods, just replace 4 oz from each 1 lb of flour with 4 oz of oats, either medium oatmeal or porridge oats. They are especially nice with rye flour – see Oatmeal Rye recipe.

HARVEST KNOT

Rye Bread

Rye bread is famous for its taste but it is a more difficult bread to make as it is very low in gluten and the result is a moist, sticky dough. For best results make rye bread with 50% rye flour and 50% wheat flour. Rye bread is especially good if made with a starter as sour dough bread, or made with added buttermilk and caraway seeds.

Sour Dough Rye

1 jam jar starter
1 lb wheat flour
1 lb rye flour
2 dsp molasses
1 tbs caraway seeds
2 tbs oil
2 tsp salt
approx. ¾ pint water

Proceed as for sour dough bread, adding the rye flour, molasses, caraway seeds and oil in the morning.

Specially Sour Rye

For extra sourness, use ½ pint buttermilk, natural yogurt or sour cream in place of half a pint of water and proceed as above.

Oatmeal Rye (2 loaves)

A light, richly flavoured bread, the heaviness of the rye balanced by the lightness of the oatmeal.

1½ oz fresh yeast or
¾ oz dried yeast
½ pt warm milk
½ pt warm water
1 tbs molasses
1 lb wheat flour
2 tsp salt
2 dsp oil
½ lb rye flour
½ lb oatmeal

Dissolve the yeast in the warm water and milk, then beat in the molasses and wheat flour. Beat well and leave to rise in a warm place.

Add the salt, oil, rye flour and oatmeal and mix to form a soft dough. Knead well then leave to rise for one hour.

Knead again then shape into two loaves, either tin or oval. Brush with milk and leave to rise in a warm place. Bake at 400°F, reg. 6 for 40–45 mins., brushing with milk again about 10 minutes before the end.

Oatmeal Rye with Caraway

Add 1 tbs caraway seeds with the salt and oil. Sprinkle liberally with caraway before baking.

Oatmeal Rye with Tang

Use ½ pint buttermilk or yogurt instead of the ½ pint of milk.

Buttermilk Rye (2 loaves)

1 lb wheat flour
1 oz fresh yeast or
½ oz dried yeast
2 dsp molasses
8 fl oz buttermilk
½ pint warm water
2 tsp salt
2 oz melted butter
1 lb rye flour

Make a batter with the wheat flour, yeast, molasses, buttermilk amd water. Beat well and leave to rise in a warm place.

Then add the remaining ingredients and mix to form a soft dough. Knead well on a floured board and then leave to rise for 45–60 minutes.

Knead again lightly and form into two loaves, either tin or oval. Leave to rise and bake for 40–45 minutes, 400°F, reg. 6. Brush with milk approximately 10 minutes before the end.

Barley Bread

Once tried, barley bread will be made again and again as it has a lovely addictive taste. Barley, being low in gluten, will not rise well on its own, but if made as ordinary bread with 50% barley and 50% wheat flour, it works really well. Or try unleavened barley bread – a Tibetan speciality.

Unleavened Barley Bread (1 large or 2 small loaves)

1¼ lb wheat flour
6 oz barley flour
2 oz sunflower seeds
2 tbs oil
1 tsp salt
1¼ pints boiling water

Roast the barley flour and sunflower seeds in the oil until golden brown –this really helps improve the flavour. Mix with the wheat flour and salt. Add the water, mixing until a dough forms, then knead lightly, keeping the hands cool in a bowl of cold water. If the dough is a bit wet, then add extra flour as you go along. Form into one large or two small loaves and put into tins. If possible, leave overnight, or for 4–6 hours, in a warm place. Then bake at 375°F, reg. 5 for 1¼–1½ hours.

Corn Bread

Traditional corn bread in the USA is more of a spoon bread, a bit like a sponge cake, delicious served with savoury bean stews and casseroles. Corn meal or flour can be used in ordinary bread recipes very successfully although it is low in gluten so it is best mixed with wheat flour. A mixture of 50% corn flour and 50% wheat flour makes a lovely golden loaf, with a rich flavour and smooth texture. Especially good with herbs added to make Herby Corn Bread and served with soups or salads.

Corn Spoon Bread

6 oz corn flour
2 oz wheat flour
1 tsp salt
2 tsp honey
2 oz melted butter or oil
2 eggs separated
approx. 10 fl oz milk

Separate the eggs and mix the yolks with the other ingredients. Beat the egg whites till fluffy and fold in. Pour into a square baking tin and bake for 40 minutes, 350°F, reg. 4.

Savoury Corn Spoon Bread

To the above recipe add 3 oz grated cheese, 1 medium onion, chopped and lightly fried and 1 tsp thyme.

Granary Bread (two cobs)

Most home-made granary bread is made with a ready mixed granary flour, which sometimes contains a proportion of white or 81% flour. Here is a recipe to make your own granary mix:

1 lb 2 oz wheat flour
6 oz rye flour
4 oz cracked wheat
1½ oz fresh yeast or
¾ oz dried yeast and 1 tsp honey
1 dsp molasses
2 dsp malt extract
2 tsp salt
2 dsp oil
¾ pint warm water

Firstly, put the cracked wheat in a dry pan and roast over a medium heat until brown and crunchy. This really improves the flavour.

Then make a batter by dissolving the yeast in the warm water (adding the honey if using dried yeast), mixing in ½ lb wheat flour and then mixing in the cracked wheat. Beat well and leave to rise in a warm place.

Then mix in the remaining ingredients (including the remaining 10 oz of wheat flour), knead lightly and leave to rise in a warm place.

When doubled in size, knead lightly and divide into two. Form into cobs (see page 30) and place on a flat baking tray or in round tins. Brush the tops with milk and sprinkle with cracked wheat. Leave to rise then bake for 45–50 minutes, 375°F, reg. 5. Leave to cool before cutting.

Mixed Grain Bread (2 loaves)

6 oz cornmeal
6 oz porridge oats
6 oz rye flour
12 oz wheat flour
1½ oz fresh yeast or
¾ oz dried yeast and 1 tsp honey
2 tsp salt
2 oz melted butter
1 tbs molasses

sesame seeds and egg yolk on top.

Pour 1 pint boiling water over the cornmeal and oats and stir in the butter and molasses. Meanwhile dissolve the yeast in just a little warm water, adding the honey if using dried yeast. When the corn and oats are warm, mix in all the ingredients to make a smooth dough, adding a little extra warm water if necessary. Knead well and then leave to rise in a warm place for 45–50 minutes.

Knead again lightly and then form into two loaves – either tins or bloomers. Brush with egg yolk then sprinkle with sesame seeds. Leave to rise in a warm place, then bake for 45 minutes, 375°F, reg. 5.

Nutritious Bread

Soft, crumbly, extra rich and nutritious.

1½ lbs wheat flour
2 oz wheat germ
4 oz soya flour
1 oz fresh yeast or
½ oz dried yeast and 1 tsp honey
2 tbs oil
2 tsp salt
1 tbs molasses
1 pint water

Dissolve the yeast (and honey if using dried yeast) in a little of the water. Then mix all the ingredients together to form a soft dough. Knead well and leave to double in size in a warm place.

Knead again lightly and form into two loaves. Brush with milk and leave to rise in a warm place. Bake for 40–45 minutes, 375°F, reg. 5.

Special Cob Recipe (2 loaves)

2 lbs wheat flour
1 oz fresh yeast or
½ oz dried yeast and 1 tsp honey
1 tbs malt extract
1 dsp molasses
2 tsp salt
18 fl oz warm water

Dissolve the yeast in a little of the warm water, adding the honey if using dried yeast. Dissolve the malt extract and molasses in the remaining warm water. Mix all the ingredients together to form a soft dough. Knead well and leave to rise in a warm place.

Knead again and form into two cobs (see page 30). Place on greased baking sheets or in round tins. Brush with milk and sprinkle with cracked wheat. Leave to rise in a warm place then bake for 45 minutes, 375°F, reg. 5.

Left-Over Unleavened Bread

A meal in a slice. Can be made with any left-overs, i.e. cooked vegetables, grains, beans, nut roasts, bean sprouts, even salads. Mix the left-overs with enough flour to form a workable, soft dough, adding a little oil, salt and milk.

Form into loaves and put into tins. If possible, leave overnight or for 4–6 hours in a warm place. Bake in the morning at 375°F, reg. 5 for 40–50 minutes.

Four Grain Unleavened Bread

8 oz wheat flour
4 oz buckwheat flour (or rye or barley)
4 oz cornmeal
2 oz soya flour
1 tsp salt
2 tbs oil
1 tbs tamari soya sauce
water to mix

Mix all the ingredients together, adding enough water to form a soft dough. Knead lightly. If possible, leave overnight in a warm place. Then knead lightly again and form into a loaf. Leave in a warm place for an hour, then bake at 375°F, reg. 5 for 50–60 minutes.

Rolls

Rolls can be made from any bread mixture, simply divide the dough into equal parts and form into rounds instead of making loaves. Put the rolls on a baking sheet and tuck the edges underneath all round – this will stop them spreading. Cover with a cloth and leave to rise, then bake at 425°F, reg. 7 for 20 minutes. These rolls do sometimes have a hard crust on them, which doesn't please everyone. One way to avoid this is to cover the rolls with a cloth as soon as they come out of the oven – the steam trapped by the cloth helps keep the crust soft. Alternatively, mix up a special dough.

Soft Bread Rolls

12 oz wheat flour
½ oz fresh yeast or
¼ oz dried yeast and 1 tsp honey
1 oz melted butter
1 beaten egg
⅓ pint warm milk

Dissolve the yeast in the warm milk, adding the 1 tsp honey if using dried yeast. Mix the flour and salt together and then add the yeast and beaten egg. Mix into a soft dough and knead lightly. Form into 8 rounds (they are quite big so do more by making them smaller if you wish) and put on a flat baking tray. Tuck the edges underneath all round to stop them spreading and leave to rise in a warm place. Then bake at 400°F, reg. 6 for 20 minutes.

Sesame Rolls

Brush each roll with milk and sprinkle liberally with sesame seeds before baking.

Fruit Rolls

Add 4 oz sultanas, 1 tbs honey and 1 tsp mixed spice to the above recipe or per pound of flour. Then brush with a mix of milk and honey before baking.

Savoury Breads

Celery Bread (1 loaf)

1 lb flour
½ oz fresh yeast or
¼ oz dried yeast and 1 tsp honey
1 tbs celery seeds
1 tsp black pepper
2 tbs tamari soya sauce
2 stalks celery, very finely chopped
1 tbs oil
just under ½ pint warm water

Dissolve the yeast in a little of the warm water, adding the 1 tsp honey if using dried yeast. Gently fry the chopped celery in the oil until transparent, then mix with the flour, celery seeds and black pepper. Add the tamari and yeast then add enough warm water to make a firm dough. Knead well and leave to rise in a warm place.

Knead again lightly then put into a tin. Brush the top with milk and sprinkle with a few celery seeds or black pepper. Leave to rise in a warm place for 30 minutes then bake for 40 minutes, 400°F, reg. 6.

Cheese Bread (1 loaf)

1 lb flour
½ oz fresh yeast or
¼ oz dried yeast and 1 tsp honey
6 oz grated cheese
½ tsp black pepper
1 tsp dried thyme
1 tbs tamari soya sauce
¼ pint warm milk
just under ¼ pint warm water

Dissolve the yeast in a little of the warm water, adding the 1 tsp honey if using dried yeast. Mix the flour, herbs, black pepper and 5 oz of the grated cheese together. Add the yeast, warm milk and tamari, then add the remaining warm water as necessary to form a firm dough. Knead lightly and leave to rise in a warm place.

Knead again and form into a loaf. Leave to rise again in a warm place for 20–30 minutes, then bake at 400°F, reg. 6 for 40 minutes. Ten minutes before the end, brush with milk and sprinkle the remaining 1 oz of cheese over the top.

Savoury Rye (2 loaves)

A lovely savoury bread, ideal with soups or for sandwiches.

1 lb wheat flour
1 oz fresh yeast or
½ oz dried yeast and 1 tsp honey
1 pint warm water
2 finely chopped and fried onions
2 tsp fennel seeds
2 tsp caraway seeds
1 tbs tamari soya sauce
2 tsp salt
2 dsp oil
1 lb rye flour

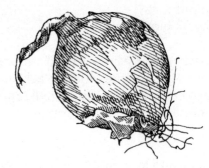

Make a thick batter by dissolving the yeast (and honey if using dried yeast) in the warm water and then mixing in the flour. Beat well and leave to rise in a warm place.

Add all the remaining ingredients and mix to form a soft dough. Knead lightly and then leave to rise for 45–60 minutes.

Knead again lightly and form into loaves. Brush with milk and sprinkle with black pepper. Leave to rise and then bake for 40 minutes, 400°F, reg. 6.

Cornish Savoury Breads

Ideal for using left-over cooked food.

Make up 1 lb of bread dough, knead and leave to rise. Have the left-over cooked food on hand, i.e. cooked vegetables, beans, stew, nut loaf, which should be cold and fairly moist, but not so it runs when a spoonful is put on a plate.

Divide the dough into small pieces and roll into fairly thin rounds. Pile the vegetable mix onto half of this round, wet the edges and fold the other half over, pinching the edges together. Brush with milk or beaten egg and prick in a couple of places with a fork.

Leave to rise for 20 minutes in a warm place then bake at 400°F, reg. 6. for 20–25 minutes.

Especially good if the dough has added herbs or grated cheese. These are lovely hot or cold – ideal for picnics or long walks.

Little Savoury Cakes

8 oz wheat flour
2 oz soya flour
2 oz melted butter or oil
2 oz grated cheese
1 beaten egg
1 tsp each oregano and marjoram
2 tbs tamari soya sauce
½ tsp black pepper
milk

Rub the butter or oil into the wheat and soya flours, then add the remaining ingredients, mixing well. Add enough milk to form a stiff dough. Roll the dough to approx. ½″ thick. Cut into 2–3″ rounds and place on a flat baking tray. Brush with milk and bake at 400°F, reg. 6 for 20–25 minutes, turning them over after 10 minutes. Slice and serve with butter while still warm. Delicious with salads or soups.

Sweet Breads and Cakes

Malt Bread

Rich, dark and moist.

1 lb flour
½ oz fresh yeast or
¼ oz dried yeast and 1 tsp honey
1 tsp salt
2 tbs malt extract
2 tbs molasses
4 oz raisins
⅓ pint warm milk

Dissolve the yeast in the warm milk, adding the 1 tsp honey if using dried yeast. Mix the flour, salt and raisins together. Heat the malt extract and molasses until runny then mix everything together well. Mix or knead lightly. Put into a 2 lb loaf tin and leave to rise in a warm place for 30 minutes. (Do not worry if it doesn't rise much at this stage – it will do in the oven.) Brush with melted honey and bake at 375°F, reg. 5 for 45–50 minutes. Allow to cool before slicing.

Banana Bread (1 loaf)

A favourite with everyone, banana bread can be elaborated further with the addition of 2 eggs, cinnamon and ginger into a banana cake, or served as it is, a sweet, moist loaf.

1 lb flour
½ oz fresh yeast or
¼ oz dried yeast and 1 tsp honey
½ tsp salt
2 tbs honey
2 large or 3 small mashed bananas
2 oz raisins or sultanas
⅓ pint warm milk

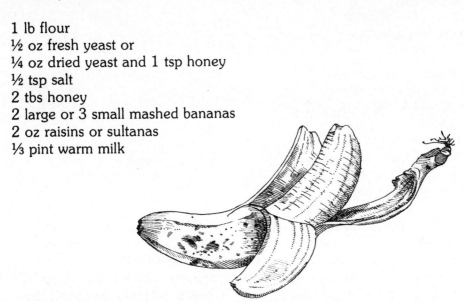

Dissolve the yeast in the warm milk with the 1 tsp honey if using dried yeast. Mix all the other ingredients together, then add the yeast, mixing well. Knead lightly, adding a little extra flour if necessary. Put into a 2 lb bread tin and leave to rise in a warm place for 25–30 minutes. Then bake for 40 minutes, 375°F, reg. 5. Ten minutes before the end, brush with milk or beaten egg and honey.

Orange Bread (1 loaf)

Fruity and tangy. Lovely with cottage cheese.

1 lb wheat flour
½ oz fresh yeast or
¼ oz dried yeast and 1 tsp honey
grated rind and juice of 1 orange
chopped fruit of 1 orange
3 oz chopped dates
1 tbs honey
⅓ pint warm water

Dissolve the yeast in the warm water, adding the honey if using dried yeast. Add all the other ingredients together, melting the honey if it is a little thick. Add the yeast mixture and mix well. Knead lightly. Put in a greased 2 lb bread tin and leave to rise in a warm place for 30 minutes or so. (Do not worry if it does not rise much at this stage – it does surprising things in the oven.) Bake at 400°F, reg. 6 for 15 minutes, then at 375°F, reg. 5 for 25 minutes.

Apricot Whirls (makes approx. 12)

Fruit filled whirls, light and sweet.

12 oz flour
½ oz fresh yeast or
¼ oz dried yeast and 1 tsp honey
1 beaten egg
1 tbs honey
⅓ pint warm milk
6 oz apricots
1 tsp cinnamon
juice of 1 lemon
1 tbs honey
a little water
egg and honey to glaze

Dissolve the yeast in the warm milk, adding the honey if using dried yeast. Then mix into the flour with the egg and honey to make a soft dough. Knead lightly and leave to rise in a warm place.

Simmer the apricots with the cinnamon, lemon juice and honey, adding water as necessary to form a thick paste.

Roll the dough out into a rectangle ¼″ thick. Spread the filling over the dough, then roll it up like a swiss roll. Cut into 1″ slices and place upright on a greased baking tray. Brush with beaten egg yolk and honey, then leave in a warm place for 15 minutes.

Bake at 400°F, reg. 6, for 20–25 minutes. Eat hot.

Prune Whirls

Use prunes instead of apricots in the above recipe.

Yeasted Fruit Cake

Traditional, sweet, light, fruity, delicious.

1 lb flour
½ oz fresh yeast or
¼ oz dried yeast
½ pint milk and water mixed and warmed
2 tbs honey
2 oz melted butter
2 beaten eggs
8 oz sultanas
1 tsp cinnamon
1 tsp mixed spice

Make a batter from half of the flour, the yeast, warm milk and water and 1 tbs of honey. Leave to rise in a warm place, for approximately 30 minutes.

Then add the butter, eggs, sultanas, remaining tbs of honey and remaining half pound of flour. Mix well to form a moist, soft dough.

Butter a round cake tin or two bread tins, put in the cake mixture and leave to rise in a warm place for 30–45 minutes. Then bake at 400°F, reg. 6 for 40–45 minutes. Allow to cool before cutting as it is very soft and will crumble if cut too soon.

For a sticky top, brush with melted honey ten minutes before the end of baking.

Fruity Scones

These scones are made with yeast instead of baking powder, so have a slightly different texture. Baking powder can be used instead, but as it is made up of a number of chemicals it is not recommended.

12 oz wheat flour
½ oz fresh yeast or
¼ oz dried yeast and 1 tsp honey
3 oz sultanas
1 tsp salt
1 tbs honey
1 oz melted butter
1 egg
¼ pint natural yogurt
2 fl oz warm water

Dissolve the yeast in the warm water, adding the 1 tsp honey if using dried yeast. Combine the flour, salt and sultanas. Combine the egg, honey, butter and yogurt together and then mix them all together with the yeast. This will make a soft dough. Knead lightly then roll the dough out to approximately ½" thick. Cut into rounds and place on a greased baking tray. Brush with milk or beaten egg and honey. Leave to rise in a warm place until its size has doubled, then bake at 425°F, reg. 7 for 15–20 minutes. Serve warm, split, with butter.

Spicy Scones

Add 1 tsp cinnamon and 1 tsp ginger for spicy scones, or as a change, try 1 tsp caraway seeds.

Plain Tea Breads

1¼ lb wheat flour
1 oz fresh yeast or
½ oz dried yeast
1 dsp malt extract
½ pint warm milk
1 tsp salt
1 beaten egg
2 oz melted butter

Make a batter with the yeast, warm milk, malt extract and 4 oz of the flour. Mix well then leave to rise in a warm place.

Add the remaining ingredients to form a soft dough. Knead lightly and leave to rise for 30 minutes. Then divide into 8 balls. Roll out slightly (into teacake shapes) and put on a flat baking tray, tucking the edges in underneath slightly. Leave to rise. Bake at 425°F, reg. 7 for 20 minutes. After 10 minutes brush with a mixture of beaten egg and melted honey for a golden and sweet glaze. Serve hot for tea.

Fruity Tea Breads

Add 3 oz sultanas and 1 tsp each cinnamon and ginger to the above mix.

4 Grain Sweet Spoon Bread

A nutty flavoured, very nutritious sponge bread. Try it with butter or with stewed fruit and yogurt as a sweet.

2 oz soya flour
4 oz corn flour
2 oz wheat flour
2 oz barley flour
1 oz fresh yeast or
½ oz dried yeast and 1 tsp honey
2 eggs
2 oz melted butter
2 tbs honey
½ pint warm water and milk mixed

Dissolve the yeast in a little of the warm water and milk, adding the 1 tsp honey if using dried yeast. Mix the flours together. Mix the butter, honey and eggs together then combine everything together and mix well. Put into a greased square cake tin and leave in a warm place for 25 minutes. Then bake at 425°F, reg. 7 for 15 minutes and then at 375°F, reg. 5 for 20 minutes.

It can then be cut into squares or spooned from the tin.

Apple and Sultana Cake

4 oz butter
2 tbs honey
2 eggs
3 oz sultanas
2 large eating apples, grated
4 tsp ginger powder
2 tsp cinnamon
a little milk
10–12 oz flour

Cream the butter and honey together then add the eggs. Add sultanas and grated apples. Combine the spices with the flour and add alternately with the milk to form a soft, creamy mix. Put into a greased and lined cake tin and bake for 40–45 minutes, 350–375°F, reg.4–5.

Carob

Carob comes from the Locust bean and is very similar in taste to cocoa, but is far richer in nutrients (iron, calcium and vitamins in particular) and is lower in fat (only 2%). Cocoa contains Tyranine, a possible cause of migraine headaches, that carob does not contain. Carob syrup has the richest flavour but use carob flour if the syrup is unobtainable.

Carob Cake

A sticky, dark, chocolate flavoured cake, delicious.

4 oz butter
3 tbs carob syrup (or 2 oz carob flour)
2 tbs honey
2 tbs molasses
3 eggs
the juice and rind of one orange
6 oz raisins
10 oz flour (8 oz if using carob flour)

Cream the butter, carob syrup, honey and molasses together. Beat in the eggs then the orange juice and rind. Add the raisins. If using carob flour then sieve well and mix in. Slowly fold in the flour.

Line one large or two small cake tins with greaseproof paper and spoon in the mixture. If making one large cake then bake for approximately 50 minutes, 350°F, reg. 4 or until firm in the middle. If making a sandwich cake then bake for 25–30 minutes, 375°F, reg. 5.

For a filling or icing, try pureed apples and dates, cooked until soft in a little orange juice and honey. Spread over the cake and sprinkle with desiccated coconut. Or puree some apricots and mix with natural yogurt for a creamy topping.

Apricot Carob Cake

Substitute 6 oz apricots, stewed in a little water until soft, for the raisins in the above recipe, and use lemon juice instead of orange. Top or fill with pureed apricots, honey and yoghurt.

Carob Brownies

2 oz butter
2 tbs honey
2 eggs
1 tsp vanilla essence
2 oz carob powder
3 oz wheat flour
2 oz walnuts
3 tbs milk

Cream butter, honey and eggs. Add vanilla essence. Sieve the carob powder and add, with the nuts. Add the flour and milk and mix well then put into a buttered square cake tin. Bake for 30 minutes, 375°F, reg. 5. Cut into squares while warm.

This is especially delicious if a layer of stewed apricots is underneath and it is served as a sweet with cream or yoghurt.

Rich Fruit Cake

4 oz butter
3 tbs honey
1 tbs molasses
2 eggs
12 oz dried fruit (apricots, figs, sultanas, etc.)
3 fl oz natural yoghurt
10–12 oz flour

Pour boiling water over the dried fruit and leave to soak. Cream the butter, honey and molasses together, then beat in the eggs. Drain the fruit, chop roughly and add, also adding the yoghurt and mixing well. Gently fold in the flour.

Line a cake tin with greaseproof paper. Spoon in the mixture and decorate with sliced almonds or walnuts. Bake for 1½ hours, 350°F, reg. 4, or until firm in the middle.

Flat Breads

Chappatis

Chappatis are probably the most well-known of Indian flat breads and are very easily made. One can buy wholewheat chappati flour, which is very finely ground, but use 100% flour instead if you can't get it.

Mix 6 oz flour with enough water to form a firm dough. Break off small amounts and roll out into very thin rounds. Cook each one in a dry frying pan (cast iron is ideal) until golden brown on both sides (a few minutes). Then pop them under the grill and they should puff up splendidly. Serve with curries or stews. They should be eaten hot as they go a bit tough when cold.

Try using buttermilk or yoghurt instead of water for a tangy chappati.

Puris

Also from India, puris are made like chappatis and then deep fried. They can be shallow fried but will not puff up so well.

Tortillas

Made with yellow corn meal, tortillas are best known in South America although they are made like chappatis. They have a lovely golden colour and very special taste. Make them in the same way as chappatis, but slightly thicker.

Nan

Another form of Indian flat bread, thicker and smaller than chappatis and baked in the oven.

Mix 12 oz flour with 1 tsp salt, 2 oz oil and just under ½ pint milk, to form a soft dough. Knead lightly and roll out into 6 rounds, approximately 1″ thick. Dust with flour and bake at 400°F, reg. 6 for 20–25 mins.

Rotis

Made with gram flour, or lentil flour, sometimes sold as Besan flour!

6 oz gram flour
1 small onion, finely chopped
¼ tsp chilli powder
½ tsp cumin seeds or powder
½ tsp salt
1 tbs melted butter or oil.

Mix all the ingredients together and add enough water or buttermilk to form a soft dough. Divide into small balls and roll out fairly thin. Cook rotis on both sides in a lightly greased heavy frying pan or griddle until golden on both sides.

Pita

Arabian flat breads, usually filled with salads or spicy bean mixes.

Make 1 lb bread dough as normal and leave to rise once. Then break the dough into 1–2″ size balls. Sprinkle with flour and leave to rise for 20 minutes. While they are rising, heat the oven to 450°F, reg. 8. This is important as it is the sudden burst of heat that makes the pitas puff up.

Roll the balls out, on a well-floured surface, into 5–6″ circles, approx. ¼″ thick. Dust with flour and place on a floured baking tray. Put them into the hot oven for 6–8 minutes. They should puff up beautifully. If you have kept the outside of the balls dry with flour then they will form a quick crust, capturing the steam inside.

Once out of the oven, either cut in half crossways and then split each half, or split the whole pita in half and serve either hot or cold with lots of filling. They can be reheated by toasting quickly.

Oatcakes

There are many different recipes for oatcakes, that were once the staple food of Scotland and the North of England, eaten instead of ordinary bread. Traditionally they were made almost like sour dough bread, with some of the oatmeal mixture being kept back each day for the next days baking. Once cooked, oatcakes can be dried out for a few minutes in the oven and will then store almost indefinitely in an air-tight container. Here are four recipes, all slightly different:

Yeasted Oatcakes

2 pints warm water
1 oz fresh yeast or
½ oz dried yeast
3 lbs fine oatmeal (as fine as possible)

Stir all the ingredients together, mixing by hand until smooth. Leave to rise in a warm place. Divide into small pieces and roll out flat, approximately ¼″ thick. Cook on both sides in a dry frying pan or griddle over a medium heat until golden brown. They can be made more crispy by baking in the oven for a further 5–10 minutes.

Poured Yeasted Oatcakes

1 pint milk and water mixed
1 oz fresh yeast or
½ oz dried yeast
6 oz fine oatmeal
3 oz flour
1 tsp salt

Mix oatmeal, flour and salt. Warm the liquid and pour in, mixing well. Sprinkle in the yeast and stir to form a smooth batter. Leave in a warm place for 20–25 minutes. Stir again. Heat and lightly grease a frying pan or griddle and pour enough batter to cover the base thinly. Cook on both sides over a medium heat until golden brown.

Plain Oatcakes

2 oz flour
8 oz oatmeal
2 tbs melted butter or oil
4–5 tbs hot water

Blend all the ingredients together with enough water to form a soft dough. Turn onto a board dusted with oatmeal. Knead lightly then roll out to approximately ¼″ thickness. Cut into rounds or wedges and place on a flat baking sheet. Bake for 20–25 minsutes, 375°F, reg. 5. Alternatively, they can be cooked in a dry frying pan or griddle over a medium heat.

Savoury Oatcakes

Especially nice with cheese.

4 oz flour
4 oz oatmeal
2 oz melted butter or oil
1 tsp herbs (oregano or thyme are nice)
1 tsp yeast extract
4–5 tbs hot water

Dissolve the yeast extract in the hot water, then mix all the ingredients together. Knead lightly then make into small balls and roll out flat. Put onto a flat baking tray and bake for 30 minutes, 325–350°F, reg. 3–4.

Pancakes, Muffins and Waffles

There are many varieties of pancakes, most are easy to make, all are fun to eat and once you have mastered the art of tossing, then they are fun to make as well.

Basic Pancake Mix

4 oz flour
1 egg
1 tsp salt
½ pint milk

Beat all the ingredients together. If possible, leave the mixture for an hour or so before using as this gives time for the flour to soften in the milk. Heat a flat-bottomed frying pan or griddle with a very small amount of butter or oil, until really hot. Cast iron pans are best but they are also rather heavy! Pour in a ladle of batter, turning the pan as you do so to ensure even coverage. Cook on a medium heat for just a few minutes, then toss or turn with a spatula and cook on the other side. Keep hot in the oven and serve hot.

Sweet Pancakes

Add 1 tbs honey to the basic mix and serve with lemon juice and honey. Or fill with pureed apricots or figs and serve with cream.

Savoury Pancakes

Add black pepper, herbs, crushed garlic, tamari soya sauce, yeast extract or anything else you fancy to the basic mix. Roll up the pancakes when cooked and serve with salad or vegetables and a sauce. Or fill with mashed beans, vegetables, cooked grains or nut roast, roll up and cover with a sauce and bake for 10 minutes.

For cheesy pancakes add 4 oz grated cheese to the basic mix.

For vegetable pancakes, add left-over cooked vegetables, chopped fine, to the basic mix, along with seasonings. These are nice if made fairly thick and spooned into the pan.

Buckwheat Pancakes

These are a delight, having quite a different taste. They are best when savoury, with added herbs and tamari. Make in the same way as the pancakes above, but replace the wheat flour with buckwheat flour. Stir the batter each time before making a pancake as the flour tends to sink to the bottom of the bowl.

Sour Dough Pancakes

Make up a batter as for the first stage of Sour Bread dough. Leave overnight and then make the pancakes from this batter. Delicious, especially with cream cheese and honey for breakfast!

Pancake Bonanza

Make a whole pile of sweet pancakes. Stew lots of apricots in lemon juice, water and honey until soft, then puree. Have some cream and cream cheese standing by.

Layer the cooked pancakes one by one with the apricot puree and cream cheese so that you have a pancake, apricots, pancake, cream cheese, pancake, apricots, pancake etc. Top with whipped cream. Put in the fridge for about 15 minutes before serving on a hot day.

Alternatively, try cream cheese blended with lots of oranges and honey, sandwiched with pancakes. Then make a hot sauce from orange juice, honey and arrowroot and pour over the top.

Scotch Pancakes or Drop Scones

I remember my grandmother making these, sizzling on a hot plate. She used white flour and white sugar, but made with wholewheat flour and honey, they not only taste as good but sizzle just as good too.

8 oz flour
2 dsp honey
2 beaten eggs
2 oz melted butter
¼ pint milk

Mix all the ingredients together to form a thick batter. Heat a griddle or heavy frying pan and lightly grease. Drop in tablespoonfuls of batter and cook on both sides, over medium heat, until golden brown. Serve hot with butter and lemon juice.

Winter Scotch Pancakes

Heavier, with extra nutrition and a fruity surprise.

6 oz flour
3 oz oat flakes or oatmeal
2 oz wheat germ
2 oz sultanas or chopped dates
2 beaten eggs
1 tbs honey
1 tsp salt
⅓–½ pint milk

Make as above, adding enough milk to form a thick batter. Cook as above.

Muffins and Waffles

Made with any blend of different flours, eggs, milk and seasonings, either sweet or savoury. Muffins are like little round cakes, baked in muffin tins, whilst waffles are made thinner and baked in a waffle tin.

Corn Muffins

4 oz corn flour
4 oz wheat flour
1 tsp salt
2 dsp honey
2 oz melted butter
2 eggs
¼ pint milk

Combine the flours and salt. Separate the eggs and combine the yolks with the honey, butter and milk. Mix together with the flour lightly. Whisk the egg whites and fold in. Bake in muffin tins for 15–20 minutes, 425°F, reg. 7. Serve hot.

English Muffins

These are slightly different as they are made with yeast and cooked in a griddle on top of the stove.

1½ lbs flour
2 tsp salt
1 oz fresh yeast or
½ oz dried yeast and 1 tsp honey
2 oz melted butter or oil
¾ pint milk and water mixed
semolina or rice flour to dust

Dissolve the yeast in half the milk/water, adding the 1 tsp honey if using dried yeast. Mix the flour and salt together and warm in the oven for ten minutes. Then add the butter, yeast and remaining liquid to form a smooth dough. Leave to rise in a warm place for 30 minutes. Then roll the dough out to approx. 1″ thick and cut into 2″–3″ rounds. Place on a flat tray sprinkled with rice flour and leave to rise in a warm place.

Heat an ungreased griddle or large frying pan and gently transfer the muffins with the aid of a palette knife. Sprinkle with rice flour and cook over a medium heat for about 7 minutes on both sides. Cool, then split, toast and serve hot.

Raisin Muffins

8 oz flour
3 oz raisins
2 oz melted butter
2 eggs
¼ pint milk

Combine the flour and raisins. Separate the eggs and combine the yolks with the honey, butter and milk. Mix lightly with the flour. Whisk the egg whites and fold in, then spoon the mixture into muffin tins. Bake at 425°F, reg. 7 for 15–20 minutes. Serve hot, split, with butter.

Pastry

Pastry made with wholewheat flour is really easy, so long as you are prepared to break all the rules in the book, like making a wet dough, kneading it or turning it over. It is easier if a soft fat is used, either soft butter or oil, rather than a hard fat, although oil does tend to make it a bit more crumbly.

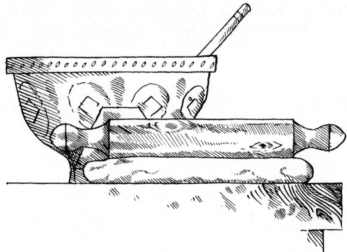

Basic Recipe:

8 oz flour
4 oz butter
1 tsp salt
3–4 tbs water

Mix the butter and salt into the flour to form 'breadcrumbs'. Add the water drop by drop, until you have a firm but quite soft dough. Err on the generous side with the water as it is easier to handle a wet dough than a dry one. Extra flour can always be added, but it is more difficult to add extra water later on.

Roll out on a floured board, kneading a little if it is still too crumbly, and adding a little extra flour if it is a bit wet. Turn the pastry round and over as much as you like, making sure it doesn't stick to the board. Get to know your pastry and don't be afraid of it! Line an 8″ pie dish by rolling the pastry onto the rolling pin and then gently rolling it off into the dish. Trim the edges.

Baking blind: This is done when the pastry is going to have a wet filling, but you don't want soggy pastry. Simply prick the bottom of the pie a few times with a fork and then bake for 10 minutes, 400°F, reg. 6.

Pastry variations

Try adding one or more of the following:

1. Grated orange or lemon rind.
2. 1 dsp fresh herbs or 2 tsp dried herbs.
3. 1 dsp sesame seeds.
4. 1 tbs ground nuts.
5. 1 dsp soya flour.
6. 3 oz grated cheese and ½ tsp black pepper.
7. 1 crushed clove of garlic and ½ tsp black pepper.
8. Substitute 2 oz oatmeal for 2 oz flour, for a crumbly, nutty flavoured pastry.

Extra Rich Pastry

For a really rich, crumbly shortcrust pastry, use 8 oz flour and 6–8 oz butter. Use enough butter so that the pastry holds together without any water and press into your pie dish instead of rolling out.

Yeasted Pastry

Easy to make, especially when making bread. Simply make an extra 8 oz
dough, roll out fairly thin to fit your pie dish, fill and bake for 25–30 minutes.
To make more luxurious, add a beaten egg and 2 oz butter to the dough.

Savoury

Add herbs, salt and pepper, or grated cheese to the dough. This sort of pastry
is traditionally used for pizza, with a filling of chopped and lightly fried
onions, sliced tomatoes or tomato puree, grated cheese, herbs and olives.

Sweet

Add 1 tbs honey and a few sweet spices to the dough. Fill with sliced apples
or pears and brush with beaten egg yolk and honey before baking. Or fill with
pureed apricots or figs, top with chopped nuts and honey then serve with
cream.

Index

94

Bibliography

Brown, Edward Espe, *The Tassajara Bread Book*, Routledge & Kegan Paul
David, Elizabeth, *English Bread and Yeast Cookery*, Penguin/Allen Lane
Deadman, Peter and Betteridge, Karen, *Nature's Foods*, Hutchinson.
TACC, *The TACC Report: Bread*, Available through PDC, 27 Clerkenwell Close, London
EC1